SCHOLASTIC

D1824040

BEST PRACTICES *in Action*

GRADES 5 & UP

Math Test Prep That Matters!

100 Standards-Based Math Prompts That Develop
Students' Critical Thinking and Deepen Their
Understanding of Key Math Concepts

JOSEPH A. PORZIO

NEW YORK • TORONTO • LONDON • AUCKLAND • SYDNEY
MEXICO CITY • NEW DELHI • HONG KONG • BUENOS AIRES

Teaching *Resources*

Cover design by Jason Robinson
Interior design by Holly Grundon
Interior illustrations by Mike Moran

ISBN-13: 978-0-439-59723-4
ISBN-10: 0-439-59723-4
Copyright © 2006 by Joseph A. Porzio
All rights reserved.
Printed in the USA.

1 2 3 4 5 6 7 8 9 10   31   15 14 13 12 11 10 09 08 07 06

Contents

Introduction

*In an age now driven by the relentless necessity
of scientific and technological advance, the current
preparation that students in the United States receive
in mathematics and science is, in a word, unacceptable.*

— Thomas L. Friedman, *The World Is Flat:
A Brief History of the Twenty-First Century*

Over the past three decades educators, business leaders, and policymakers calling for education reform have voiced deep concerns over our students' mathematics and science achievement (Clements, Sarama, & DiBiase, 2004). These concerns seem especially justified when we compare our students' scores on international tests, such as Trends in International Mathematics and Science Study (TIMSS), with those of students from other nations. In 2003, U.S. fourth-grade students ranked 12th out of 25 countries in math scores (International Association for the Evaluation of Educational Achievement, TIMSS, 2003).

In 1983, the U.S. Department of Education published the report "A Nation at Risk," often cited as the origin of current reform efforts. GOALS 2000, signed into law on March 31, 1994, listed a series of ambitious goals, which includes making the United States "first in the world in mathematics and science education." Even the National Assessment of Educational Progress (NAEP), the "Nation's Report Card," prompts repeated calls for reform. Just after the start of the new millennium, the federal government, through the No Child Left Behind Act (NCLB), expanded its role in education by establishing accountability and certification requirements that affected students, educators, and public schools across America. In his January 2006 State of the Union address, President George W. Bush announced ". . . an American Competitiveness Initiative to give our nation's children a firm grounding in math and science."

Clearly, there is more attention and recognition of the importance of mathematics (Kilpatrick, Swafford, & Findell, 2001) in a global economy where the vast majority of jobs require more sophisticated skills than jobs in the past required.

How can we—as regional/district leaders, site supervisors of mathematics, math coaches, classroom teachers, support staff in after-school academic intervention services, and parents—respond to the recognized needs in a manner that will lead to greater academic achievement in mathematics for all students?

Scholastic's Best Practices in Action series provides a definitive response to the call for action from those concerned with promoting and supporting challenging and rigorous classroom instructional practices, rooted in scientifically and/or evidence-based research. The series features promising best practices that impact teaching and learning by ensuring alignment between standards, assessment, and instruction. Among its key features is the recognition that clear, well-defined standards (what students are expected to know and be able to do at their grade level) have a positive impact on classroom teachers' instruction and students' learning.

The Mathematical Sciences Education Board's report "Everybody Counts" (1989) states: "We must ensure that tests measure what is of value, not just what is easy to test. If we want students to investigate, explore, and discover, assessment must not measure just mimicry mathematics." Further, the six key principles in the National Council of Teachers of Mathematics (NCTM) *Principles and Standards for School Mathematics* describe specific features of high-quality mathematics education. Educators who know the value of integrating content and process standards are eager to find supportive resources that complement their mathematics program.

Math Test Prep That Matters! fulfills this need and features a collection of challenging activities designed to promote thinking and foster communication through development of mathematical language (process standards) while enhancing mathematical concepts and their related skills (content standards). This book was written in direct response to the increased attention in mathematics, including that in the formative early childhood years where early childhood educators—the foundation builders—are developing students' understanding of mathematical concepts and their related skills. The challenges found in *Math Test Prep That Matters!* provide opportunities for investigations and rigorous activities that are based in content and designed to promote thinking and oral and written communication skills.

What Does It Mean to Be Proficient in Mathematics?

While we have witnessed profound swings during the past years in what it means to be successful in mathematics (e.g., new math, back to basics, NCTM's Agenda for Action which focused on problem solving), we now recognize that math proficiency requires much more than facility in using computational procedures in arithmetic.

In November 2004, the New York State Education Department's Mathematics Standards Committee presented its recommendations to the New York State Board of Regents, based upon numerous references, including *Principles and Standards for School Mathematics* (NCTM, 2000), *Adding It Up: Helping Children Learn Mathematics* (National Research Council, 2001), *Engaging Young Children in Mathematics: Standards for Early Childhood Mathematics Education* (Lawrence Erlbaum Associates, 2004), and *The Math We Need to "Know" and "Do"* (Corwin Press, 2000). The committee recognized that "every teacher of mathematics, whether at the elementary, middle, or high school level, has an individual goal to provide students with the knowledge and understanding of the mathematics necessary to function in a world that is very dependent upon the application of mathematics. Instructionally, this goal translates into three components:

1. Conceptual understanding
2. Procedural fluency
3. Problem solving"

These components are integrally related and need to be taught simultaneously and should be a component of every lesson.

From Research to Practice

How does *Math Test Prep That Matters!* support, complement, and improve student achievement in mathematics in the classroom?

• It promotes the use of promising instructional practices that are rooted in scientifically/ evidence-based research, as defined in the U.S. Department of Education's website at www.ed.gov and its link to the What Works Clearinghouse. (NOTE: On May 15th, 2006, U.S. Secretary of Education Margaret Spellings announced the names of seventeen expert panelists to comprise the National Mathematics Advisory Panel. The panel's findings and determinations in the area of mathematics will serve as a basis for building capacity and proficiency in the area of mathematics.)

• It develops conceptual understanding and their related skills while promoting communication, reasoning, and thinking. Focusing instruction on the meaningful development of important mathematical ideas increases the level of student understanding (Brownell, 1945). There is a long history of research on the effects of teaching for meaning and understanding.

• It provides several opportunities through the graphic prompts for students to invent new knowledge through non-routine problems. Teachers should periodically introduce a lesson involving a new skill by posing it as a problem to be solved and regularly allow students to build new knowledge based on their intuitive knowledge and informal procedures. Students learn both concepts and skills by solving problems (Cobb, 1991).

• It stimulates whole-class discussion following individual and group work. In addition to promoting communication, this serves as an effective diagnostic tool. Research suggests that teachers should provide opportunities such as activities, problems, and assignments for students to interact (i.e., work in small groups and share ideas) in problem-rich situations (Davidson, 1985).

More Research to Support the Use of Math Test Prep That Matters!

• Teaching math with a focus on number sense encourages students to become problem solvers in a wide variety of situations and to view mathematics as a discipline that is important (Markovits & Sowder, 1994; Cobb, 1991).

- Long-term use of concrete materials is positively related to increases in student mathematics achievement and improved attitudes towards mathematics (Suydam & Higgins, 1977; Driscoll, 1990). In a recent meta-analysis of sixty studies (kindergarten through post-secondary) that compared the effects of using concrete materials with the effects of more abstract instruction, Sowell (1989) found that long-term use of concrete materials by teachers knowledgeable in their use improved student achievement and attitudes. John van de Walle's translation model demonstrates how we can develop understanding from one external representation of an idea to another (van de Walle, 1998; Lesh, Post, & Behr, 1987).

- Numerous studies of mathematics achievement at different grade and ability levels show that students benefit when real objects (manipulatives) are used as aids in learning mathematics (Bennett, 1986).

- *EDThoughts: What We Know About Mathematics Teaching and Learning* offers numerous citings related to effective instructional methods where time is allotted for students to individually ponder appropriate strategies; identify necessary tools to assist in solving the problem; work in small groups exploring and discussing ideas and solving the problem; and report their findings to the class (Sutton, 2002).

How to Use This Book

The standards-based prompts in this book are arranged by the content and process strands typically found in an NCTM standards-based curriculum. The prompts feature graphics similar to those in student texts and on formative and normative assessments, further supporting the alignment of standards, assessment, and instruction. Offer these graphic prompts only after you have instructed students on the basic concepts using practices that include hands-on/concrete manipulatives, models, and representations (Sowell, 1989).

The graphic prompts are designed so that students can easily recognize the content area highlighted and then develop a written and/or oral response to the graphic. This strategy helps build students' content knowledge (conceptual understanding and their related skills) while developing and strengthening their process skills (i.e., problem solving, reasoning and proof, oral and written communication, connections, and representation). The graphic prompts across all content and process strands are designed to promote thinking, reasoning, problem solving, and oral and written communication (Sutton, 2002).

After students have shared their responses to a graphic prompt, you may wish to offer a challenge or extension related to the same prompt. Embedded assessment helps you determine a student's level of understanding of content based upon his or her responses. Following are some examples of how you can use the graphic prompts to assess students' learning and further challenge them:

Number and Operations

Page 17: Students should be able to recognize and define *prime numbers*—positive integers that have exactly two factors. Make sure students understand that the number 1 is NOT a prime number since it has only one factor. Students might ask how the Sieve of Eratosthenes works. Challenge them to learn more about Eratosthenes (276–194 BC) and his "sieve." Ask them: *Why do you think this method of identifying prime numbers is called a "sieve"? Which numbers are screened out?* Invite them to visit the websites www.nctm.org and www.mathforum.org to investigate Eratosthenes as well as prime and composite numbers.

Algebra

Page 29: Students may notice that quadrants A, B, and C are related. Guide them to understand how the formula for the perimeter of a rectangle is derived. Ask students to create a gridded model of a 3-by-6-inch rectangle, then have them work in pairs or small groups to model, demonstrate, and explain how the formula for area is derived. As an extension, challenge students to investigate and explain how the information in quadrant D can be used to find the area and circumference of a circle.

Geometry

Page 34: Review the Pythagorean theorem with students, prompting them to think about how they can model the formula $a^2 + b^2 = c^2$. One way is to place 9 centimeter squares or a 3-by-3-cm grid below the base of the triangle. Next to the 4-centimeter leg, students can place 16 centimeter squares or a 4-by-4-cm grid. Along the hypotenuse, they can place 25 centimeter squares or a 5-by-5-cm grid. The result would be: $3^2 + 4^2 = 5^2$ or $9 + 16 = 25$.

Measurement

Page 44: Guide students to recognize the two circles and rectangle as the parts that make up a cylinder. Challenge students to work in pairs or small groups to derive, explain, and use the formula for a cylinder's surface area ($SA = 2\pi r^2 + 2\pi rh$) and its volume ($V = \pi r^2 h$).

Data Analysis and Probability

Page 48: Encourage students to explore different ways of showing data, like the box plot on this page. If necessary, help them read the data. Explain that the box itself contains the middle 50 percent of the data. The right edge of the box represents the 75th percentile of the data, while the left edge of the box represents the 25th percentile. The center line is the median. The ends of the line represent the minimum and maximum values of the data. Students might ask questions about the different values represented by the box plot. Challenge students to

collect data or use previously collected data to create their own box plot.

Problem Solving

Page 52: A typical question students might ask would be: *How many handshakes were exchanged?* Invite students to come up with various strategies to solve this handshaking problem. For example, they might break it down into a simpler problem (e.g., two people shaking hands is one handshake, three people shaking hands is three handshakes, and so on). Students could also work in pairs or small groups to act out the problem, draw a picture or model, or create a chart or table. Challenge students to derive a formula for finding the number of handshakes between 6, 10, 25, and 50 parents!

Reasoning and Proof

Page 56: If necessary, point out the units of measurement in the sums at the end of each row and column. Explain that each shape represents a value and that they have to be added horizontally and vertically. Students might ask: *What's the best place to begin figuring out the values? (Since the first column is made up of all circles, simply divide 1 meter by 4 to come up with 25 centimeters, the value of the circle.)* Challenge students to create a similar 3 x 3 model or even a 4 x 4 model.

Communication

Pages 58–59: Invite students to conduct research on any of the suggested topics (or on other related topics) and share their findings with the class. You can have them work individually, in pairs, or in small groups.

Connections

Pages 60–61: Challenge students to discover math outside math class. Obviously math is used in science, but do students realize that it's also used in social studies (e.g., maps and scales), in literature (e.g., patterns in poetry), even in physical education (e.g., time and rates)? Encourage students to present to the class examples of where they find math in the real world.

Representation

Page 63: Encourage students to work in pairs or small groups to explore and investigate the possible outcomes of rolling three number cubes. You might want to show them how to start a chart or table to record their observations. For example:

Cube #1 (1–6)	Cube #2 (1–6)	Cube #3 (1–6)
1	1	1
1	1	2
1	1	3
1	1	4
1	1	5
1	1	6

Bibliography

Resources for Developing, Supporting, and Strengthening Mathematical Proficiency

Bennett, W. J. (1986). *What works: Research about teaching and learning.* Washington, DC: United States Department of Education.

Broad Prize for Urban Education. (2002). *Showcasing success/Rewarding achievement.* Austin, TX: National Center for Educational Accountability.

Brownell, W. A. (1945). When is arithmetic meaningful? *Journal of Education Research, 38,* 481–498.

Clements, D. H., Sarama, J., & DiBiase, A.-M. (Eds.). (2004). *Engaging young children in mathematics: Standards for early childhood mathematics education.* Mahwah, NJ: Erlbaum.

Cobb, P. et al. (1991). Assessment of a problem-centered second-grade mathematics project. *Journal for Research in Mathematics Education, 22,* 3–29.

Davidson, N. (1985). Small-group cooperative learning in mathematics: A selective view of the research. In R. Hertz-Lazarowitz, S. Kagan, S. Sharan, R. Slavin, & C. Webb (Eds.), *Learning to Cooperate, Cooperating to Learn* (pp. 211–230). New York: Plenum.

Driscoll, M. J. (1982). *Research within reach: Elementary school mathematics.* Reston, VA: National Council of Teachers of Mathematics.

Driscoll, M. J. (1990). The teacher's role: Manipulatives from The bridge from concrete to abstract. In M. J. Driscoll, *Research within reach: Elementary school mathematics* (6th printing). Reston, VA: National Council of Teachers of Mathematics.

Friedman, T. L. (2005). *The world is flat: A brief history of the twenty-first century.* New York: Farrar, Straus & Giroux.

GOALS 2000: Educate America Act. (1994, March 31). Pub. Law 103-227 (108 Stat.125)

Kilpatrick, J., Swafford, J., & Findell, B. (Eds.). (2001). *Adding it up: Helping children learn mathematics.* Washington, DC: National Academy Press.

Lesh, R. A., Post, T. R., & Behr, M. J. (1987). Representations and translations among representations in mathematics learning and problem solving." In C. Janvier (Ed.), *Problems of representation in the teaching and learning of mathematics* (pp. 33–40). Hillsdale, NJ: Erlbaum.

Markovits, Z., & Sowder, J. (1994). Developing number sense: An intervention study in grade 7. *Journal for Research in Mathematics Education, 25,* 4–29.

National Research Council. (1989). *Everybody counts: A report to the nation on the future of mathematics education.* Washington, DC: National Academies Press

National Assessment of Educational Progress (NAEP). National Center for Educational Statistics. Institute of Educational Sciences. United States Department of Education. http://nces.ed.gov/nationsreportcard/

National Commission of Excellence in Education. (1983). *A nation at risk: The imperative for educational reform.* Washington, DC: U.S. Government Printing Office.

New York State Education Department. (2005, March). *Mathematics core curriculum.* http://www.emsc.nysed.gov /ciai/mst/mathstandards/revised3.htm

Principles and standards for school mathematics. (2000). Reston, VA: National Council of Teachers of Mathematics.

Solomon, P. G. (2000). *The math we need to "know" and "do": Content standards for elementary and middle grades.* Thousand Oaks, CA: Corwin Press.

Sowell, E. J. (1989). Effects of manipulative materials in mathematics instruction. *Journal for Research in Mathematics Education, 20,* 409–505.

Stenmark, J. K. (Ed.). (1991). *Mathematics assessment: Myths, models, good questions and practical suggestions.* Reston, VA: National Council of Teachers of Mathematics.

Sutton, J., & Krueger, A. (Eds.). (2002). *EDThoughts: What we know about mathematics teaching and learning.* Aurora: CO: Mid-Continental Research for Education and Learning.

Suydam, M. N., & Higgins, J. L. (1977). *Activity-based learning in elementary school mathematics: Recommendations from research.* Columbus, OH: ERIC/Clearinghouse for Science, Mathematics, and Environmental Education.

Trends in International Mathematics and Science Study. International Association for the Evaluation of Educational Achievement. U.S. Department of Education. http://nces.ed.gov/timss/

Van de Walle, J. A. (1998). *Elementary and middle school mathematics: Teaching developmentally* (3rd ed.). New York: Addison Wesley Longman.

NCTM Standards

Standard – Instructional programs from Pre-kindergarten through Grade 12 should enable all students to:	Expectations – In Grades 6-8, all students should:
I: Number and Operations	
A. Understand numbers, ways of representing numbers, relationships among numbers, and number systems	1. Work flexibly with fractions, decimals, and percents to solve problems; 2. Compare and order fractions, decimals, and percents efficiently and find their approximate locations on a number line; 3. Develop meaning for percents greater than 100 and less than 1; 4. Understand and use ratios and proportions to represent quantitative relationships; 5. Develop an understanding of large numbers and recognize and appropriately use exponential, scientific, and calculator notation; 6. Use factors, multiples, prime factorization, and relatively prime numbers to solve problems; 7. Develop meaning for integers and represent and compare quantities with them.
B. Understand meanings of operations and how they relate to one another	1. Understand the meaning and effects of arithmetic operations with fractions, decimals, and integers; 2. Use the associative and commutative properties of addition and multiplication and the distributive property of multiplication over addition to simplify computations with integers, fractions, and decimals; 3. Understand and use the inverse relationships of addition and subtraction, multiplication and division, and squaring and finding square roots to simplify computations and solve problems.
C. Compute fluently and make reasonable estimates	1. Select appropriate methods and tools for computing with fractions and decimals from among mental computation, estimation, calculators or computers, and paper and pencil, depending on the situation, and apply the selected methods; 2. Develop and analyze algorithms for computing with fractions, decimals, and integers and develop fluency in their use; 3. Develop and use strategies to estimate the results of rational-number computations and judge the reasonableness of the results; 4. Develop, analyze, and explain methods for solving problems involving proportions, such as scaling and finding equivalent ratios.
II. Algebra	
A. Understand patterns, relations, and functions	1. Represent, analyze, and generalize a variety of patterns with tables, graphs, words, and, when possible, symbolic rules; 2. Relate and compare different forms of representation for a relationship; 3. Identify functions as linear or nonlinear and contrast their properties from tables, graphs, or equations.
B. Represent and analyze mathematical situations and structures using algebraic symbols	1. Develop an initial conceptual understanding of different uses of variables; 2. Explore relationships between symbolic expressions and graphs of lines, paying particular attention to the meaning of intercept and slope; 3. Use symbolic algebra to represent situations and to solve problems, especially those that involve linear relationships; 4. Recognize and generate equivalent forms for simple algebraic expressions and solve linear equations.
C. Use mathematical models to represent and understand quantitative relationships	1. Model and solve contextualized problems using various representations, such as graphs, tables, and equations.
D. Analyze change in various contexts	1. Use graphs to analyze the nature of changes in quantities in linear relationships.
III. Geometry	
A. Analyze characteristics and properties of two- and three-dimensional geometric shapes and develop mathematical arguments about geometric relationships	1. Precisely describe, classify, and understand relationships among types of two- and three-dimensional objects using their defining properties; 2. Understand relationships among the angles, side lengths, perimeters, areas, and volumes of similar objects; 3. Create and critique inductive and deductive arguments concerning geometric ideas and relationships, such as congruence, similarity, and the Pythagorean relationship.

Standard – Instructional programs from Pre-kindergarten through Grade 12 should enable all students to:	Expectations – In Grades 3–5, all students should:	
B. Specify locations and describe spatial relationships using coordinate geometry and other representational systems	1. Use coordinate geometry to represent and examine the properties of geometric shapes; 2. Use coordinate geometry to examine special geometric shapes, such as regular polygons or those with pairs of parallel or perpendicular sides.	**III. Geometry**
C. Apply transformations and use symmetry to analyze mathematical situations	1. Describe sizes, positions, and orientations of shapes under informal transformations such as flips, turns, slides, and scaling; 2. Examine the congruence, similarity, and line or rotational symmetry of objects using transformations.	
D. Use visualization, spatial reasoning, and geometric modeling to solve problems	1. Draw geometric objects with specified properties, such as side lengths or angle measures; 2. Use two-dimensional representations of three-dimensional objects to visualize and solve problems such as those involving surface area and volume; 3. Use visual tools such as networks to represent and solve problems; 4. Use geometric models to represent and explain numerical and algebraic relationships; 5. Recognize and apply geometric ideas and relationships in areas outside the mathematics classroom, such as art, science, and everyday life.	
A. Understand measurable attributes of objects and the units, systems, and processes of measurement	1. Understand both metric and customary systems of measurement; 2. Understand relationships among units and convert from one unit to another within the same system; 3. Understand, select, and use units of appropriate size and type to measure angles, perimeter, area, surface area, and volume.	**IV. Measurement**
B. Apply appropriate techniques, tools, and formulas to determine measurements	1. Use common benchmarks to select appropriate methods for estimating measurements; 2. Select and apply techniques and tools to accurately find length, area, volume, and angle measures to appropriate levels of precision; 3. Develop and use formulas to determine the circumference of circles and the area of triangles, parallelograms, trapezoids, and circles and develop strategies to find the area of more-complex shapes; 4. Develop strategies to determine the surface area and volume of selected prisms, pyramids, and cylinders; 5. Solve problems involving scale factors, using ratio and proportion; 6. Solve simple problems involving rates and derived measurements for such attributes as velocity and density.	
A. Formulate questions that can be addressed with data and collect, organize, and display relevant data to answer them	1. Formulate questions, design studies, and collect data about a characteristic shared by two populations or different characteristics within one population; 2. Select, create, and use appropriate graphical representations of data, including histograms, box plots, and scatterplots.	**V. Data Analysis and Probability**
B. Select and use appropriate statistical methods to analyze data	1. Find, use, and interpret measures of center and spread, including mean and interquartile range; 2. Discuss and understand the correspondence between data sets and their graphical representations, especially histograms, stem-and-leaf plots, box plots, and scatterplots.	
C. Develop and evaluate inferences and predictions that are based on data	1. Use observations about differences between two or more samples to make conjectures about the populations from which the samples were taken; 2. Make conjectures about possible relationships between two characteristics of a sample on the basis of scatterplots of the data and approximate lines of fit; 3. Use conjectures to formulate new questions and plan new studies to answer them.	
D. Understand and apply basic concepts of probability	1. Understand and use appropriate terminology to describe complementary and mutually exclusive events; 2. Use proportionality and a basic understanding of probability to make and test conjectures about the results of experiments and simulations; 3. Compute probabilities for simple compound events, using such methods as organized lists, tree diagrams, and area models.	

	Standard – Instructional programs from Pre-kindergarten through Grade 12 should enable all students to:
VI. Problem Solving	**A.** Build new mathematical knowledge through problem solving;
	B. Solve problems that arise in mathematics and in other contexts;
	C. Apply and adapt a variety of appropriate strategies to solve problems;
	D. Monitor and reflect on the process of mathematical problem solving.
VII. Reasoning and Proof	**A.** Recognize reasoning and proof as fundamental aspects of mathematics;
	B. Make and investigate mathematical conjectures;
	C. Develop and evaluate mathematical arguments and proofs;
	D. Select and use various types of reasoning and methods of proof.
VIII. Communication	**A.** Organize and consolidate their mathematical thinking through communication;
	B. Communicate their mathematical thinking coherently and clearly to peers, teachers, and others;
	C. Analyze and evaluate the mathematical thinking and strategies of others;
	D. Use the language of mathematics to express mathematical ideas precisely.
IX. Connections	**A.** Recognize and use connections among mathematical ideas;
	B. Understand how mathematical ideas interconnect and build on one another to produce a coherent whole;
	C. Recognize and apply mathematics in contexts outside of mathematics.
X. Representation	**A.** Create and use representations to organize, record, and communicate mathematical ideas;
	B. Select, apply, and translate among mathematical representations to solve problems;
	C. Use representations to model and interpret physical, social, and mathematical phenomena.

* Standards notation on activity pages:
S: I A / E: 1 means the activity meets the Number & Operations (I)
Standard A (Understand numbers, ways of representing numbers, . . .),
Expectation 1 (Work flexibly with fractions, . . .).

Name: _____   Date: _____

$95.00
15% discount

$110.00
20% discount

1. Write about what you see above.

_____

_____

2. Ask a question about it.

_____

_____

3. Answer your question.

_____

_____

Name: _____   Date: _____

A	B
0.125	$12 \frac{1}{2} \%$
C	D
$\frac{1}{8}$	$1.25

1. Write about what you see above.

_____

_____

2. Ask a question about it.

_____

_____

3. Answer your question.

_____

_____

Number and Operations

Name: _____   Date: _____

B

D

A

C

1. Write about what you see above.

_____

_____

2. Ask a question about it.

_____

_____

3. Answer your question.

_____

_____

Number and Operations

Name: _____   Date: _____

Percent

0   25%   A   B   100%

Fraction

0   C $\frac{1}{2}$ D   1

Decimal

0   E   F   0.75   1.0

1. Write about what you see above.

_____

_____

2. Ask a question about it.

_____

_____

3. Answer your question.

_____

_____

Name: _____ Date: _____

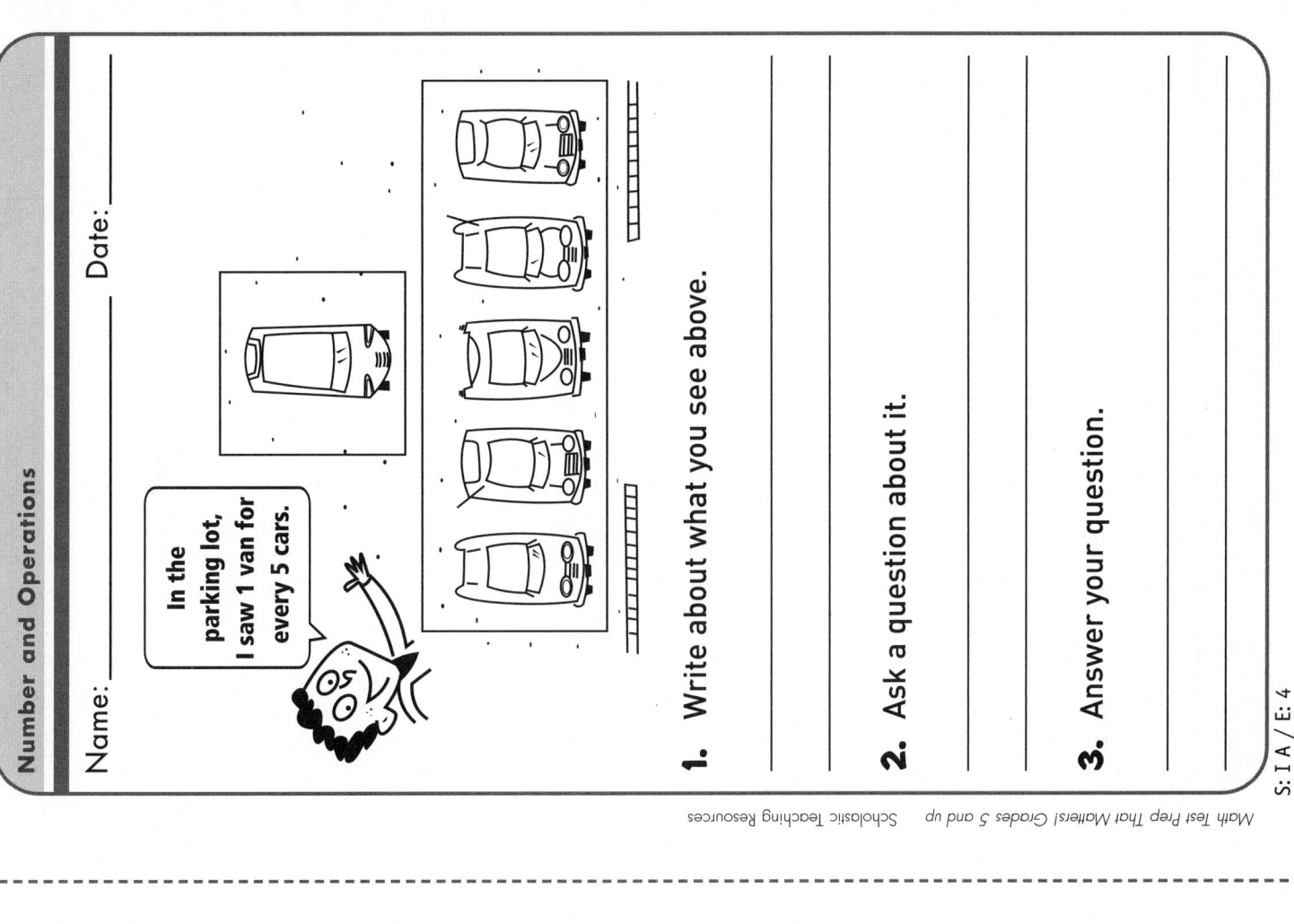

Speech bubble: In the parking lot, I saw 1 van for every 5 cars.

1. Write about what you see above.

_____

2. Ask a question about it.

_____

3. Answer your question.

_____

S: I A / E: 4

Name: _____ Date: _____

Speech bubble: For every coat sold, Mr. James earns $24.

Number of Coats Sold	1	2	3	4	5	6	7	...	10
Dollars Earned	$24	$48	$72					...	

1. Write about what you see above.

_____

2. Ask a question about it.

_____

3. Answer your question.

_____

S: I A / E: 4

Number and Operations

Name: _____ Date: _____

A 9.4 × 10²	**B** 9.4 × 100
C 9.4 × 20	**D** 940

1. Write about what you see above.

_____

2. Ask a question about it.

_____

3. Answer your question.

_____

Number and Operations

Name: _____ Date: _____

A 2 cm 2 cm 2 cm	**B** 2 cm 2 cm
C 2 × 2 × 2	**D** 2^3

1. Write about what you see above.

_____

2. Ask a question about it.

_____

3. Answer your question.

_____

Name: _____ Date: _____

The Sieve of Eratosthenes

② ③ ④ ⑤ ⑥ ⑦ 8̸ 9̸ 1̸0̸
⑪ 1̸2̸ ⑬ 1̸4̸ 1̸5̸ 1̸6̸ ⑰ 1̸8̸ ⑲ 2̸0̸
2̸1̸ 2̸2̸ ㉓ 2̸4̸ 2̸5̸ 2̸6̸ 2̸7̸ 2̸8̸ ㉙ 3̸0̸
㉛ 3̸2̸ 3̸3̸ 3̸4̸ 3̸5̸ 3̸6̸ ㊲ 3̸8̸ 3̸9̸ 4̸0̸
㊶ 4̸2̸ ㊸ 4̸4̸ 4̸5̸ 4̸6̸ ㊼ 4̸8̸ 4̸9̸ 5̸0̸
5̸1̸ 5̸2̸ ㊾ 5̸4̸ 5̸5̸ 5̸6̸ 5̸7̸ 5̸8̸ ㊾ 6̸0̸

Circled numbers = prime numbers

Slashed numbers = composite numbers

1. Write about what you see above.

_____

2. Ask a question about it.

_____

3. Answer your question.

_____

S: I A / E: 6

Name: _____ Date: _____

72
  8   9
    4   3   ○
  ○   2
    ○

1. Write about what you see above.

_____

2. Ask a question about it.

_____

3. Answer your question.

_____

S: I A / E: 6

Name: _____   Date: _____

A

-5

+3

-3 -2 -1   0   1   2   3   4

3 + (−5) = ☐

B

-7

+4

-3 -2 -1   0   1   2   3   4

☐

1. Write about what you see above.

_____
_____

2. Ask a question about it.

_____
_____

3. Answer your question.

_____
_____

Math Test Prep That Matters! Grades 5 and up   Scholastic Teaching Resources

S: I A / E: 7

Name: _____   Date: _____

A ● ● ● ●   **B** ● ● ● ○

C ○ ○ ○ ○   **D** ● ● ● ○

-7 -6 -5 -4 -3 -2 -1   0   1   2   3   4   5   6   7

Key
● = positive integer   ○ = negative integer

1. Write about what you see above.

_____
_____

2. Ask a question about it.

_____
_____

3. Answer your question.

_____
_____

Name: _____ Date: _____

SALE TAKE 1/3 OFF

$174.00

1. Write about what you see above.

_____

_____

2. Ask a question about it.

_____

_____

3. Answer your question.

_____

_____

S: I B / E: 1

Name: _____ Date: _____

$$\frac{4}{6}, \frac{1}{4}, \frac{7}{8}, \frac{4}{5}, \frac{2}{3}$$

1. Write about what you see above.

_____

_____

2. Ask a question about it.

_____

_____

3. Answer your question.

_____

_____

S: I B / E: 1

Name: _____ Date: _____

Associative $(a + b) + c = a + (b + c)$

$a \times (b \times c) = (a \times b) \times c$

Commutative $x + y = y + x$

$x * y * z = y * x * z$

1. Write about what you see above.

2. Ask a question about it.

3. Answer your question.

S: I B / E: 2

Name: _____ Date: _____

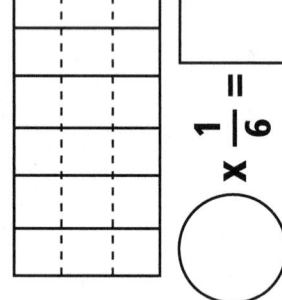

A   B

$\frac{1}{2} \times \frac{1}{4} =$ ☐

☐ $\times \frac{1}{6} =$ ◯

1. Write about what you see above.

2. Ask a question about it.

3. Answer your question.

S: I B / E: 1

Name: _____   Date: _____

8,		, 17
8 + [ ] = 17	[ ] = 17	17 − [ ] = 8
[ ] + 8 = 17	17 − 8 = [ ]	

7,		, 56
7 × [ ] = 56	[ ] = 56	56 ÷ [ ] = 7
[ ] × 7 = 56	56 ÷ 7 = [ ]	

1. Write about what you see above.

_____

2. Ask a question about it.

_____

3. Answer your question.

_____

S: I B / E: 3

Name: _____   Date: _____

Distributive Property of
Multiplication Over Addition

$$4 \times (3 + 5) = (4 \times 3) + (4 \times 5)$$

1. Write about what you see above.

_____

2. Ask a question about it.

_____

3. Answer your question.

_____

S: I B / E: 2

Number and Operations

Name: _____ Date: _____

CHEESE
$ 2.80/
POUND

1. Write about what you see above.

_____

_____

2. Ask a question about it.

_____

_____

3. Answer your question.

_____

_____

S: I C / E: 1

Number and Operations

Name: _____ Date: _____

Use a calculator to find the square root of a number between any two perfect squares. Estimate first!

Perfect Squares	1	4	9	16	25	36	49	64		
Square Roots	1	2	3	4	5	6			9	10

1. Write about what you see above.

_____

_____

2. Ask a question about it.

_____

_____

3. Answer your question.

_____

_____

S: I B / E: 3

Name: _____ Date: _____

A
one whole

0.5

0.4

$0.5 \times 0.4 =$ ☐

B
one whole

0.3

☐

1. Write about what you see above.

_____

_____

2. Ask a question about it.

_____

_____

3. Answer your question.

_____

_____

S: I C / E: 1, 2

Name: _____ Date: _____

Partitive

$.20$
$3\overline{)\,.60}$
$.6$

Subtractive

$.12\overline{)\,.60}$

1. Write about what you see above.

_____

_____

2. Ask a question about it.

_____

_____

3. Answer your question.

_____

_____

S: I C / E: 1, 2

Name: _____   Date: _____

One of these is NOT like the others! Hint: Is it a terminating or a non-terminating decimal?

A $\frac{9}{15}$	B $\frac{5}{6}$
C $\frac{7}{20}$	D $\frac{3}{4}$

1. Write about what you see above.

_____

2. Ask a question about it.

_____

3. Answer your question.

_____

S: I C / E: 3

Name: _____   Date: _____

A   B   C   D

0   1   2   3

1. Write about what you see above.

_____

2. Ask a question about it.

_____

3. Answer your question.

_____

S: I C / E: 3

Name: _____   Date: _____

A	B
$\frac{40}{90}$	40 : 50

C	D
$\frac{50}{90}$	$\frac{90}{50}$

(center: pig image — 40 dimes 50 quarters)

1. Write about what you see above.

_____

2. Ask a question about it.

_____

3. Answer your question.

_____

S: I C / E: 4

Name: _____   Date: _____

Number of Oranges	1	2	3	4	. . .	12
Cost of Oranges				$1.20		

1. Write about what you see above.

_____

2. Ask a question about it.

_____

3. Answer your question.

_____

S: I C / E: 4

Name: _____ Date: _____

CIRCUS TICKETS
1 dozen tickets = $90.00
25 tickets = $125.00

1. Write about what you see above.

_____
_____

2. Ask a question about it.

_____
_____

3. Answer your question.

_____
_____

S: I C / E: 4

Name: _____ Date: _____

Fencing the Rectangular Garden

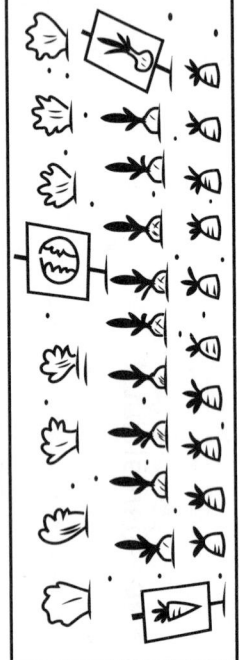

3 cm

9 cm

Scale: 1 cm = 5.3 m

1. Write about what you see above.

_____
_____

2. Ask a question about it.

_____
_____

3. Answer your question.

_____
_____

S: I C / F: 4

Name: _____   Date: _____

Filling the 500-Gallon Water Tower

Gallons: 500, 450, 400, 350, 300, 250, 200, 150, 100, 50, 0

Hours: 1 2 3 4 5 6 7 8 9 10

1. Write about what you see above.

_____

_____

2. Ask a question about it.

_____

_____

3. Answer your question.

_____

_____

S: II A / E: 2

Name: _____   Date: _____

Term	1	2	3	4	5	6
Model	□	⊞				
Square Number	1	4	9	16		

1. Write about what you see above.

_____

_____

2. Ask a question about it.

_____

_____

3. Answer your question.

_____

_____

S: II A / E: 1

Name: _____ Date: _____

Mowing the Lawn

Time in Hours	Cost to Rent Lawn Mower
1	$5
2	$10
3	$15
4	

Cost = T ($5)

Time in Hours
10 9 8 7 6 5 4 3 2 1 0

$5 $10 $15 $20 $25 $30 $35 $40 $45 $50

Cost

1. Write about what you see above.

_____
_____

2. Ask a question about it.

_____
_____

3. Answer your question.

_____
_____

S: II A / E: 3

Name: _____ Date: _____

Contributions to the Family Picnic

Number of Families	Amount Collected
1	$25
2	$50
3	$75
4	
5	
6	
...	
10	

Amount Collected

$300 $275 $250 $225 $200 $175 $150 $125 $100 $75 $50 $25 0

1 2 3 4 5 6 7 8 9 10

Number of Families

1. Write about what you see above.

_____
_____

2. Ask a question about it.

_____
_____

3. Answer your question.

_____
_____

S: II A / E: 3

Name: _____ Date: _____

A	B
$A = lw$	rectangle: 6 ft. × 3 ft.
C	D
$P = 2l + 2w$	circle: 7 cm

1. Write about what you see above.

_____

2. Ask a question about it.

_____

3. Answer your question.

_____

S: II B / E: 1

Name: _____ Date: _____

Graph the parking lots' prices.

No. of Hours	1	2	3	4	5	6	7	8
Safety Parking	$10	$12	$14	$16	$18			
OK Parking	$4	$8	$12	$16		$24		

1. Write about what you see above.

_____

2. Ask a question about it.

_____

3. Answer your question.

_____

S: II B / E: 1

Name: _____   Date: _____

Plants Around the Garden

If we doubled the size of the garden, how many plants would there be?

1. Write about what you see above.

_____
_____

2. Ask a question about it.

_____
_____

3. Answer your question.

_____

S: II B / E: 4

Name: _____   Date: _____

A	B
$3(x) + 9 = 24$	$A = lw$
C	D
$A = \dfrac{1}{2}bh$	$x = 6y$

1. Write about what you see above.

_____
_____

2. Ask a question about it.

_____
_____

3. Answer your question.

_____

S: II B / E: 3

Name: _____   Date: _____

Measuring Rectangles in Centimeters

Length	1	2	3	4
Width	24	12	8	
Area	24	24		24
Perimeter				

1. Write about what you see above.

_____

_____

2. Ask a question about it.

_____

_____

3. Answer your question.

_____

_____

Name: _____   Date: _____

Trailer Rental (week)

Plan A: Daily Weekday Rates = $10.00
Plan B: Sat. and Sun. Rates = $25.00 each day.

1. Write about what you see above.

_____

_____

2. Ask a question about it.

_____

_____

3. Answer your question.

_____

_____

Geometry

Name: _____ Date: _____

1. **Write about what you see above.**

_____

_____

2. **Ask a question about it.**

_____

3. **Answer your question.**

_____

Geometry

Name: _____ Date: _____

1. **Write about what you see above.**

_____

_____

2. **Ask a question about it.**

_____

3. **Answer your question.**

_____

Name: _____ Date: _____

Kinds of Triangles

equilateral

isosceles

obtuse

scalene

acute

right

1. Write about what you see above.

_____

_____

2. Ask a question about it.

_____

3. Answer your question.

_____

Name: _____ Date: _____

3 cm, 5 cm, 4 cm (triangle XYZ)

B, C — 48 cm, 36 cm, A, D (rectangle)

G — 10 cm, I, 8 cm, 6 cm, H

D — 16 cm, 16 cm, 6 cm, E, F

A — 12 cm, 12 cm, 4 cm, B, C

F, G — 30 cm, 40 cm, E, H (rectangle)

1. Write about what you see above.

_____

_____

2. Ask a question about it.

_____

3. Answer your question.

_____

Name: _____   Date: _____

1. Write about what you see above.

_____

_____

2. Ask a question about it.

_____

_____

3. Answer your question.

_____

_____

S: III B / E: 1

Math Test Prep That Matters! Grades 5 and up   Scholastic Teaching Resources

---

Name: _____   Date: _____

4 cm

3 cm

Create a model using manipulatives to demonstrate and explain the Pythagorean theorem.

1. Write about what you see above.

_____

_____

2. Ask a question about it.

_____

_____

3. Answer your question.

_____

_____

Name: _____ Date: _____

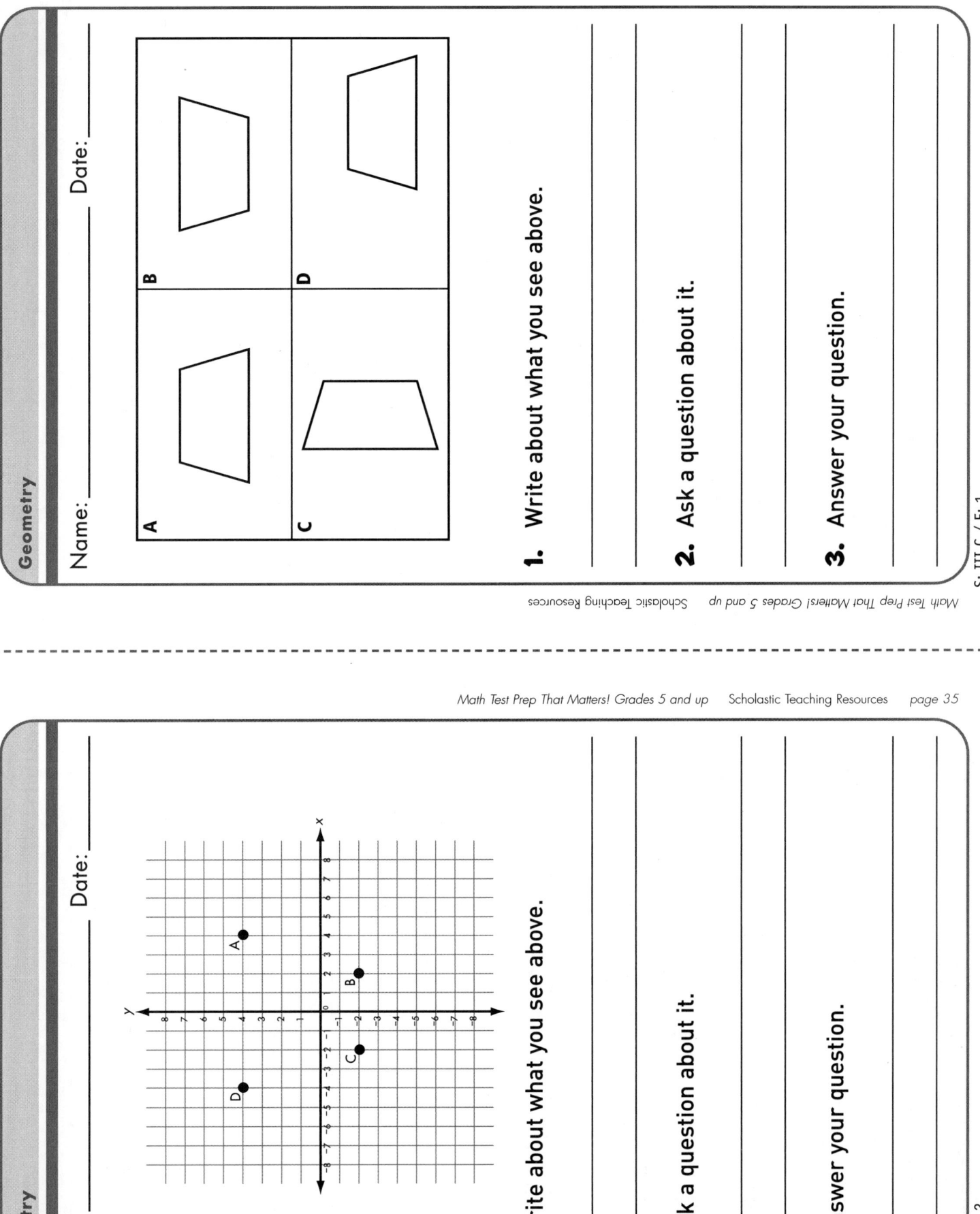

1. Write about what you see above.

_____

_____

2. Ask a question about it.

_____

_____

3. Answer your question.

_____

_____

S: III C / E: 1

Name: _____ Date: _____

1. Write about what you see above.

_____

_____

2. Ask a question about it.

_____

_____

3. Answer your question.

_____

_____

S: III B / E: 2

Name: _____ Date: _____

Use math tools to construct and explain one of the following figures:

1. Write about what you see above.

   _____

   _____

2. Ask a question about it.

   _____

   _____

3. Answer your question.

   _____

   _____

S: III D / E: 1

Name: _____ Date: _____

Use pentominoes on grid paper to model and demonstrate the following:

- congruence
- line symmetry
- rotational symmetry

1. Write about what you see above.

   _____

   _____

2. Ask a question about it.

   _____

   _____

3. Answer your question.

   _____

   _____

S: III C / E: 2

Name: _____ Date: _____

Draw a scale model to help you find the volume and surface area of a rectangular solid that measures

1.5 m x 3.0 m x 6.0 m =

1. Write about what you see above.

_____

_____

2. Ask a question about it.

_____

3. Answer your question.

_____

_____

S: III D / E: 2

Math Test Prep That Matters! Grades 5 and up   Scholastic Teaching Resources

---

Name: _____ Date: _____

Bridges of Konigsburg

Can you cross all seven bridges without crossing any bridge more than once?

C

A

D

B

1. Write about what you see above.

_____

_____

2. Ask a question about it.

_____

3. Answer your question.

_____

_____

Name: _____   Date: _____

12 ft

8 ft

4 ft

12 ft

24 ft

36 ft

1. Write about what you see above.

_____

_____

2. Ask a question about it.

_____

_____

3. Answer your question.

_____

_____

Name: _____   Date: _____

A   B   C   D

Circle	A	B	C	D
Radius				3 cm
Diameter	5 cm	3 cm	4 cm	
Circumference				

1. Write about what you see above.

_____

_____

2. Ask a question about it.

_____

_____

3. Answer your question.

_____

_____

Name: _____   Date: _____

A   **B**

Baseball

Investigate

Geometry All
Around Us

C

The Golden Rectangle

D

The Solar System

1. Write about what you see above.

_____

_____

2. Ask a question about it.

_____

_____

3. Answer your question.

_____

_____

S: III D / E: 5

Math Test Prep That Matters! Grades 5 and up   Scholastic Teaching Resources

---

Name: _____   Date: _____

**Make a building out of six cubes.
Look at the pictures below to help you
figure out what it looks like.**

Front View   Top View   Left Side View

1. Write about what you see above.

_____

_____

2. Ask a question about it.

_____

_____

3. Answer your question.

_____

_____

Math Test Prep That Matters! Grades 5 and up   Scholastic Teaching Resources   page 39

S: III D / E: 5

Name: _____   Date: _____

Prefixes and Roots
of Metric Units of Measure

Root Prefix	meter	liter	gram
milli-	0.001 meter	0.001 liter	
centi-		0.01 liter	0.01 gram
kilo-	1,000 meters		1,000 grams

1. Write about what you see above.

_____

_____

2. Ask a question about it.

_____

_____

3. Answer your question.

_____

_____

- -

Name: _____   Date: _____

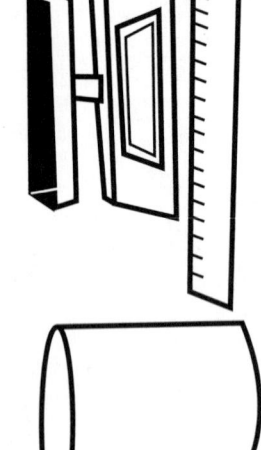

Customary Conversion

- **inch, foot, yard, mile**
- **cup, pint, quart, gallon**
- **ounce, pound, ton**

1. Write about what you see above.

_____

_____

2. Ask a question about it.

_____

_____

3. Answer your question.

_____

_____

Name: _____   Date: _____

Block	hexagon	trapezoid	rhombus	triangle
Angles				
Perimeter				
Area				
Sum of interior angles				

1. Write about what you see above.

_____

_____

2. Ask a question about it.

_____

_____

3. Answer your question.

_____

_____

S: IV A / E: 3

Name: _____   Date: _____

Heights of Students

Estimate then measure the height of several classmates.

Name	cm	m
Carlos	162	
Mindy	151	
Alicia		1.58
Byron	168	
Marta		1.53

1. Write about what you see above.

_____

_____

2. Ask a question about it.

_____

_____

3. Answer your question.

_____

_____

S: IV A / E: 2

Name: _____ Date: _____

Construct a Cube

You'll need: tag board, scissors, compass

1. Draw a circle with a radius of 7.1 cm.

2. Divide the circle into equal fourths by drawing two diameters.

3. Connect the diameters' points on the circumference so that you have four chords.

4. Score the chords so that you have sharp, crisp folds.

5. Make five more "faces" for your cube.

6. Join the faces at the folds with rubber cement.

1. Write about what you see above.

_____

_____

2. Ask a question about it.

_____

3. Answer your question.

_____

S: IV B / E: 2

Name: _____ Date: _____

How do you measure . . .

• the thickness of a coin

• the size of a dollar bill

• the distance from New York City to Washington, D.C.

• the serving you get in a fruit drink

• the liquid in an eyedropper

1. Write about what you see above.

_____

_____

2. Ask a question about it.

_____

3. Answer your question.

_____

S: IV B / E: 1

Name: _____ Date: _____

B
C
A
D

Starting with a rectangle, find the area of a parallelogram.

1. Write about what you see above.

_____

_____

2. Ask a question about it.

_____

_____

3. Answer your question.

_____

_____

S: IV B / E: 3

Name: _____ Date: _____

Find the area of a triangle.

1. Write about what you see above.

_____

_____

2. Ask a question about it.

_____

_____

3. Answer your question.

_____

_____

S: IV B / E: 3

Name: _____ Date: _____

Measuring Round Up!

Measure everything you see that is round. Use a string to measure the circumference. Measure the diameter. Collect and analyze your data on a chart or table. Look for a pattern in the relationship between the diameter and circumference.

1. Write about what you see above.

_____

_____

2. Ask a question about it.

_____

_____

3. Answer your question.

_____

_____

S: IV B / E: 3

Name: _____ Date: _____

d

c

h

h

d

1. Write about what you see above.

_____

_____

2. Ask a question about it.

_____

_____

3. Answer your question.

_____

_____

S: IV B / E: 4

Name: _____ Date: _____

18 in.

6 in.

15 cm

10 cm

2 m

6 m

4 m

1. Write about what you see above.

_____

_____

2. Ask a question about it.

_____

_____

3. Answer your question.

_____

_____

S: IV B / E: 4

Name: _____ Date: _____

B

4 cm

A

5 cm

C

1 cm

D

4 cm

E

Key					
cm	0	1	2	3	4	5
km	0	12	24	36	48	60

1. Write about what you see above.

_____

_____

2. Ask a question about it.

_____

_____

3. Answer your question.

_____

_____

S: IV B / E: 5

Name: _____   Date: _____

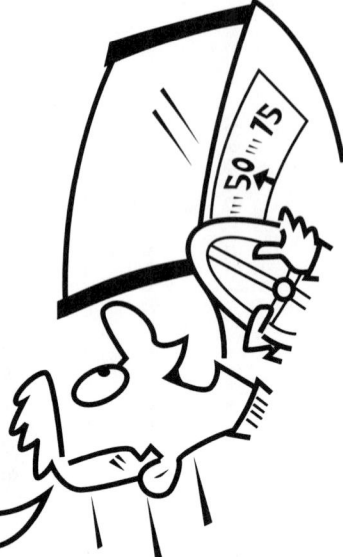

A driver travels at an average of 50 miles per hour for 4 hours and 30 minutes. Use a chart, table, or formula to explain the distance the driver traveled.

1. Write about what you see above.

_____

_____

2. Ask a question about it.

_____

_____

3. Answer your question.

_____

_____

S: IV B / E: 6

Name: _____   Date: _____

1. Fill a container with marbles.

2. Estimate how many marbles fit inside, then count them. Record your findings on the chart below.

3. Next, fill the same container with an object slightly larger than a marble. Repeat step 2.

4. Finally, fill the same container with an object smaller than a marble. Repeat step 2.

Object	Estimate	Count	Difference
marbles			

1. Write about what you see above.

_____

_____

2. Ask a question about it.

_____

_____

3. Answer your question.

_____

_____

S: IV B / E: 6

Name: _____   Date: _____

Stem-and-Leaf Plot Test Scores

3	8 7
4	5
5	6
6	7 8 3
7	0 8 4 9 5 3 0 6 4
8	3 3 5 3 5 8 7
9	4 1 3 8

1. Write about what you see above.

_____

_____

2. Ask a question about it.

_____

_____

3. Answer your question.

_____

_____

S: V A / E: 2

Name: _____   Date: _____

How We Get to School

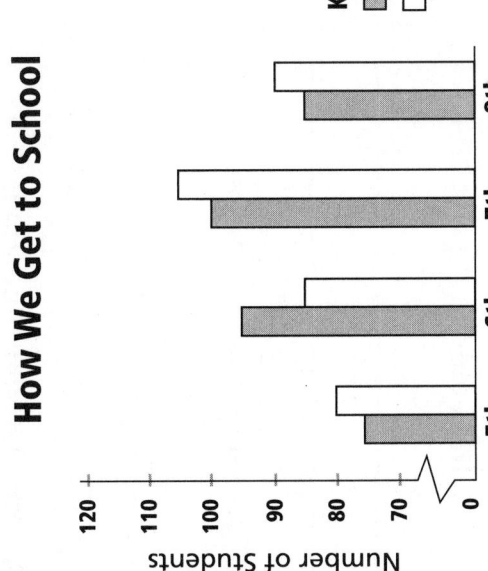

Key
- ride the bus
- walk to school

Number of Students / Grade

1. Write about what you see above.

_____

_____

2. Ask a question about it.

_____

_____

3. Answer your question.

_____

_____

S: V A / E: 1

Name: _____ Date: _____

Number of Cans Each Student Collected for the Food Drive

3	30	46	70
20	36	50	76
20	38	56	78
24	42	64	280

1. Write about what you see above.

   _____

   _____

2. Ask a question about it.

   _____

   _____

3. Answer your question.

   _____

   _____

S: V B / E: 1

Name: _____ Date: _____

Stamps in a Collector's Book

100   150   200   250   300

1. Write about what you see above.

   _____

   _____

2. Ask a question about it.

   _____

   _____

3. Answer your question.

   _____

   _____

S: V A / E: 2

Name: _____ Date: _____

Test Scores

How else could you display the data?

1. Write about what you see above.

_____

_____

2. Ask a question about it.

_____

_____

3. Answer your question.

_____

_____

S: V B / E: 2

- -

Name: _____ Date: _____

Math Test Scores and Study Time

1. Write about what you see above.

_____

_____

2. Ask a question about it.

_____

_____

3. Answer your question.

_____

_____

S: V B / E: 2

Data Analysis and Probability

Name: _____ Date: _____

You have two pennies in a cup. What are some possible outcomes if you shake the cup and toss the pennies on the desk? What if you did it 10 times, 20 times, and 100 times?

1. Write about what you see above.

_____
_____

2. Ask a question about it.

_____
_____

3. Answer your question.

_____
_____

S: V D / E: 1, 2, 3

Data Analysis and Probability

Name: _____ Date: _____

Compare the arm spans and heights of students at two different grade levels in your school. Then organize your data on a scatter plot.

1. Write about what you see above.

_____
_____

2. Ask a question about it.

_____
_____

3. Answer your question.

_____
_____

S: V C / E: 1, 2

Name: _____   Date: _____

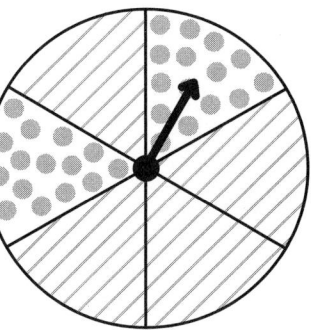

What is the probability that you would spin polka dots both times when you spin two times in a row?

1. **Write about what you see above.**

   _____
   _____

2. **Ask a question about it.**

   _____
   _____

3. **Answer your question.**

   _____
   _____

S: V D / E: 1, 2, 3

Name: _____   Date: _____

1	2	3	4	5	6	7	8	9	10
11	12	13	14	15	16	17	18	19	20
21	22	23	24	25	26	27	28	29	30
31	32	33	34	35	36	37	38	39	40
41	42	43	44	45	46	47	48	49	50
51	52	53	54	55	56	57	58	59	60
61	62	63	64	65	66	67	68	69	70
71	72	73	74	75	76	77	78	79	80
81	82	83	84	85	86	87	88	89	90
91	92	93	94	95	96	97	98	99	100

Close your eyes and point to a number on the hundred chart. What is the probability that your finger will land on a multiple of 3? What is the probability that it will land on a number that is NOT a multiple of 3?

1. **Write about what you see above.**

   _____
   _____

2. **Ask a question about it.**

   _____
   _____

3. **Answer your question.**

   _____
   _____

S: V D / E: 1, 2, 3

Name: _____   Date: _____

How many squares are there on a checkerboard? HINT: There are 5 squares in a 2 x 2 section.

1. Write about what you see above.

_____

_____

2. Ask a question about it.

_____

3. Answer your question.

_____

_____

S: VI A, B, C, D

Name: _____   Date: _____

At the end of a school meeting, each parent shook hands with the other parents and then left.

1. Write about what you see above.

_____

_____

2. Ask a question about it.

_____

3. Answer your question.

_____

_____

S: VI A, B, C, D

Name: _____   Date: _____

The Pentomino Investigation

Pentominoes are shapes that can be constructed from five squares. Each square must have at least one side in common with another square.

Challenge: Use all pentomino pieces to cover a rectangular 6 × 10, 5 × 12, or 4 × 15 area.

S: VI A, B, C, D

Name: _____   Date: _____

The Palindrome Investigation

A palindrome is a word, phrase, or number that reads the same forward and backward; for example, noon, "Madam, I'm Adam," or 32,423.

You can form a number palindrome by choosing a number (e.g., 57) and adding its reverse to it (57 + 75 = 132), then adding the reverse of its sum again (132 + 231 = 363). This particular example is called a "two-step palindrome" because it took two steps for the number to become a palindrome.

Find out the number of steps required for a number on the hundred chart to become a palindrome. Is the number a one-step, two-step, or three-step palindrome? Look for patterns in one-step, two-step, and three-step palindromes. Color-code the patterns you discover!

1	2	3	4	5	6	7	8	9	10
11	12	13	14	15	16	17	18	19	20
21	22	23	24	25	26	27	28	29	30
31	32	33	34	35	36	37	38	39	40
41	42	43	44	45	46	47	48	49	50
51	52	53	54	55	56	57	58	59	60
61	62	63	64	65	66	67	68	69	70
71	72	73	74	75	76	77	78	79	80
81	82	83	84	85	86	87	88	89	90
91	92	93	94	95	96	97	98	99	100

S: VI A, B, C, D

Name: _____ Date: _____

The Magic Square

Arrange the digits 1 to 9 on the grid so that the numbers add up to 15 vertically, horizontally, and diagonally. Use each digit only once.

1. Write about what you see above.

_____

_____

2. Ask a question about it.

_____

_____

3. Answer your question.

_____

_____

S: VI A, B, C, D

Name: _____ Date: _____

The Cylinder Investigation

Roll a piece of legal-size paper ($8\frac{1}{2}$ by 14 inches) into a long cylinder. Next, roll the same piece of legal-size paper into a short cylinder. Which cylinder holds more?

14"

$8\frac{1}{2}$"

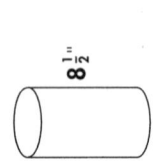

14"

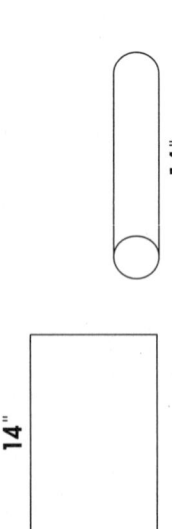

$8\frac{1}{2}$"

1. Write about what you see above.

_____

_____

2. Ask a question about it.

_____

_____

3. Answer your question.

_____

_____

S: VI A, B, C, D

Name: _____ Date: _____

Triangular Numbers	★ 1	★ ★ ★ 3	★ ★ ★ ★ ★ ★ 6	★ ★ ★ ★ ★ ★ ★ ★ ★ ★ 10
Square Numbers	★ 1	★ ★ ★ ★ 4	★ ★ ★ ★ ★ ★ ★ ★ ★ 9	★ ★ ★ ★ ★ ★ ★ ★ ★ ★ ★ ★ ★ ★ ★ ★ 16

1. Write about what you see above.

_____

_____

2. Ask a question about it.

_____

_____

3. Answer your question.

_____

_____

S: VI A, B, C, D

Name: _____ Date: _____

The Perfect Pie

The Delicious Pie Bakery baked 360 pies for the holiday. Not all were perfect. Every third pie was too cooked. Every fourth pie was cracked. Every fifth pie was too sweet. Every sixth pie was NOT sweet enough.

1. Write about what you see above.

_____

_____

2. Ask a question about it.

_____

_____

3. Answer your question.

_____

_____

S: VI A, B, C, D

Name: _____   Date: _____

HINT: Each shape is an addend.

				Sum
⬡	△	☆	⬡	29
☐	⬡	△	☆	27
☐	○	○	⬡	20
☆	☆	☆	☆	24
Sum	26	25	26	23

1. Write about what you see above.

_____

2. Ask a question about it.

_____

3. Answer your question.

_____

S: VII A, B, C, D

Name: _____   Date: _____

HINT: Each shape is an addend.

				Sum
○	△	⬡	☐	1.25 m
○	☆	☐	△	155 cm
○	☐	○	☐	2 m
○	⬡	☆	△	900 mm
Sum	1 m	140 cm	150 cm	1.8 m

1. Write about what you see above.

_____

2. Ask a question about it.

_____

3. Answer your question.

_____

S: VII A, B, C, D

Name: _____   Date: _____

1. Write about what you see above.

_____

2. Ask a question about it.

_____

3. Answer your question.

_____

S: VII A, B, C, D

Name: _____   Date: _____

1. Write about what you see above.

_____

2. Ask a question about it.

_____

3. Answer your question.

_____

S: VII A, B, C, D

Name: _____ Date: _____

Visit the Library

Read a Book

Visit the library and look for a book related to a math topic, such as the history of the metric system, money, number systems, or careers in mathematics. Write a book report and share your research with your classmates.

S: VIII A, B, C, D

Name: _____ Date: _____

Visit the Library

Read a Book

Famous Mathematicians

Visit the library and read a book about a famous mathematician, such as:

- Benjamin Banneker
- Bernoulli
- Eratosthenes
- Blaise Pascal
- Ptolemy
- Pythagoras
- Srinivasa Ramanujan
- Galileo
- Sophie Germain

- Archimedes
- John Napier
- Hypatia
- Euclid
- Isaac Newton
- Albert Einstein
- Carl Friedrich Gauss
- Leonardo Fibonacci

S: VIII A, B, C, D

Name: _____

Date: _____

Multicultural Mathematics

Read about the math contributions made by people from different cultures around the world. Share your findings about one group's contribution with your classmates.

S: VIII A, B, C, D

Name: _____

Date: _____

Mathematics: Just for the Fun of It!

Have you ever thought of mathematics as a hobby? Visit the library and read about the many math puzzles, tricks, and fun problems you can share with classmates, family, and friends.

S: VIII A, B, C, D

Name: _____ Date: _____

Create two different scale drawings of the same object—one in which the object's size is reduced, and another where its size is enlarged.

HINT: Think about ratio and proportion!

1. Write about what you see above.

   _____

   _____

2. Ask a question about it.

   _____

   _____

3. Answer your question.

   _____

   _____

Name: _____ Date: _____

Create your own word problems using the information below:

- 2.5 pounds of fish cost $4.50 per pound
- 8 ounces of wool cost $2.75
- 5 pounds of nails cost $2.30

1. Write about what you see above.

   _____

   _____

2. Ask a question about it.

   _____

   _____

3. Answer your question.

   _____

   _____

Name: _____   Date: _____

Math in the Real World

Find the connection between mathematics and the real world. Conduct research and report on how math is related to one of the following topics:

- sports
- newspaper
- music
- nature (Fibonacci)
- architecture
- cooking
- art
- marathons
- games
- bus/train schedules

S: IX C

Name: _____   Date: _____

Conduct research to find out more about:

- the golden ratio
- the golden rectangle
- the Fibonacci series

0, 1, 1, 2, 3, 5, 8, 13, 21, . . .

Use models to show how these three important math concepts are related. Show examples of where we can find these in architecture, design, art, and nature.

S: IX A, B, C

Look at different types of television programs, such as the news, a weekly show, or a variety show. Create a chart or graph that compares the amount of time given to the actual show to the amount of time used for advertisements.

Math Test Prep That Matters! Grades 5 and up   Scholastic Teaching Resources

S: X A, B, C

Use a scale drawing to construct a model of your home, school, neighborhood building, or a famous landmark. Share your project with your classmates.

Use a model to show the total number of axes of symmetry in a cube. HINT: Explore its faces, edges, and vertices.

S: X C

Math Test Prep That Matters! Grades 5 and up   Scholastic Teaching Resources

---

Use a chart, table, or other representations to record the possible outcomes of rolling three number cubes, each numbered 1 to 6.

Create Your Own

Name: _____ Date: _____

1. Write about what you see above.

   _____
   _____

2. Ask a question about it.

   _____

3. Answer your question.

   _____

Create Your Own

Name: _____ Date: _____

1. Write about what you see above.

   _____
   _____

2. Ask a question about it.

   _____

3. Answer your question.

   _____